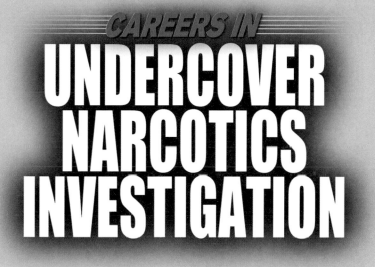

CAREERS IN

UNDERCOVER NARCOTICS INVESTIGATION

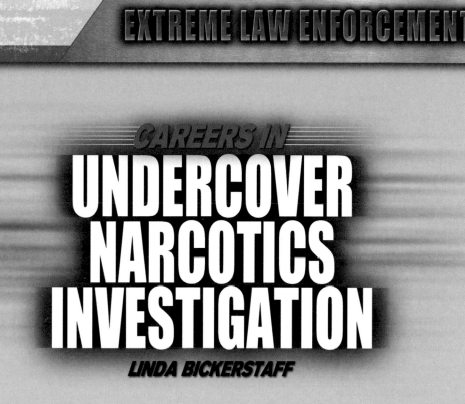

CAREERS IN
UNDERCOVER
NARCOTICS
INVESTIGATION

LINDA BICKERSTAFF

ROSEN
PUBLISHING®

New York

Published in 2014 by The Rosen Publishing Group, Inc.
29 East 21st Street, New York, NY 10010

Copyright © 2014 by The Rosen Publishing Group, Inc.

First Edition

Library of Congress Cataloging-in-Publication Data

Bickerstaff, Linda.
Careers in undercover narcotics investigation/Linda Bickerstaff.
    pages cm.—(Extreme law enforcement)
Includes bibliographical references and index.
ISBN 978-1-4777-1707-3 (library binding)
1. Drug traffic—Investigation—Vocational guidance. I. Title.
HV8079.N3B525 2014
363.25'977023—dc23

                                                      2013010906

Manufactured in the United States of America

CPSIA Compliance Information: Batch #W14YA: For further information, contact Rosen Publishing, New York, New York, at 1-800-237-9932.

CONTENTS

INTRODUCTION

The job of law enforcement officer is listed among the ten most dangerous jobs in the United States by the Bureau of Labor Statistics (BLS). It is number five on the list of the ten most stressful jobs of 2012 in a survey conducted by CareerCast.com. Undercover narcotics investigators are law enforcement officers extraordinaire. Their jobs are extremely dangerous, and the stress they encounter is unimaginable. Danger! Stress! Why would anyone want such a job? Lew Rice, a retired Drug Enforcement Administration (DEA) Special Agent, in his book *DEA Special Agent: My Life on the Front Line* gives a very simple answer: "I've always believed that undercover work is a very special occupation filled with men and women who just want to make a difference. They join this profession simply to help their fellow citizens."

Among law enforcement officers, the word "narcotic" is frequently used to mean any illegal drug. True narcotics, such as opium, heroin, and morphine, are only a few of the drugs used illegally in the United States. Drug investigators deal with all dangerous and illegal drugs, not just narcotics. To comply with common usage, the word "narcotics" will be used here to refer to all illegal drugs unless specified otherwise.

Narcotics investigators, commonly called agents, are police officers, working for local or state police or sheriff's

6

Narcotics agents working for police departments and sheriffs' offices frequently work with Special Agents from the Drug Enforcement Administration (DEA) to make major drug busts, as they did in this international investigation called Operation Raw Deal.

departments. At the federal level, agents working for the DEA have this job. They are called Special Agents rather than narcotics agents. When narcotics agents or Special Agents assume new identities for the purpose of gaining the trust of an individual or of organizations suspected of breaking drug laws, they are known as undercover agents.

The job of narcotics investigators, at all levels of government, is to enforce laws pertaining to dangerous drugs. Although it sounds simple, nothing could be further from the truth. It takes an extraordinary amount of knowledge, training, skill, personal integrity, and courage to do the job. Paul E. Doyle, a retired DEA Special Agent, in the introduction to his memoir *Hot Shots and Heavy Hits*, describes the life of an undercover agent with these words: "The greed, violence, danger, and secrecy of the illegal drug business permeate an agent's life. An agent must pretend to be someone he (or she) is not. He assumes an untraceable criminal identity; his driver's license, passport, and Social Security cards are issued under false names. A successful undercover agent plays the part so well that he actually becomes the character he is portraying. He learns to 'talk the talk' and 'walk the walk'...The risks are great."

Careers as narcotics agents are not suited to everyone. People who find undercover narcotics investigation careers most rewarding are those who want to make a positive difference in people's lives. They must be controlled risk-takers who can follow orders and handle the unexpected with flair and imagination. They will benefit greatly by being able to handle stress and frustration creatively. They must be able to commit to the job come what may. Above all else, these people must be courageous and have an incredible amount of personal integrity. If you have these qualifications, perhaps being an undercover narcotics investigator is in your future.

CHAPTER ONE

UNDERCOVER NARCOTICS INVESTIGATORS: AN OVERVIEW

Choosing the right career is one of the hardest and most important tasks a person undertakes in his or her lifetime. It pays big dividends to consider several possibilities before making any decisions. People with an interest in law enforcement careers may want to consider becoming narcotics investigators. Finding out who narcotics investigators are, what they do, and what their motivations are for doing their jobs is a good introduction to this profession.

Investigators Are Law Enforcement Officers

Narcotics agents are police officers that undergo training in police academies and work on local police forces, for county sheriff's departments, or for state police organizations. Police officers who want to be narcotics agents spend three to six years taking specialized training courses over and above those taken by other members of their organizations. They

Training at the DEA Academy in Quantico, Virginia, prepares Special Agents for deployment to Afghanistan. They will assist Afghanistan's Counter Narcotics Police in investigations targeting heroin labs and opium storage facilities.

also get on-the-job training (OJT) by working with experienced narcotics agents within their departments. After receiving the appropriate training, police officers or sheriff's deputies may be promoted to narcotics investigator positions.

Federal narcotics investigators work for the DEA, a branch of the U.S. Department of Justice. DEA Special Agents are almost always college graduates. Many have advanced degrees. They train at the DEA Academy in Quantico, Virginia. They, like narcotics agents at the local and state levels, learn the skills necessary to be successful undercover agents during the course of their training.

Investigators Enforce Drug Laws

Narcotics agents investigate illegal drug activities in cities and counties within their states to

DEA Special Agents work with antidrug agents in many foreign countries. Here, a DEA agent *(right)* participates in a training exercise with antidrug agents near Santa Rosa, Guatemala.

enforce drug laws. These investigations involve video surveillance and the use of wiretaps and other electronic information-gathering tools. When needed, agents go undercover to blend into gangs or other groups where illegal drug activity is suspected. Arrests resulting from these investigations usually lead to charges for possession of dangerous drugs.

At the federal level, Special Agents use undercover investigations to gather information and hard evidence to support the arrests of those who break federal drug laws. They also work in many foreign countries to prevent the movement of drugs from those countries into the United States. Most of the arrests made by

ALEX SALINAS, UNDERCOVER AGENT

Alex Salinas became an undercover narcotics agent one day after becoming a cop. Because this twenty-two-year-old police rookie wore braces on his teeth and looked like a high school kid, the Exeter, California, chief of police asked him to help with an undercover operation to investigate a drug ring operating in two California high schools. After only three weeks of special training with narcotics agents, Salinas, as Johnny Ramirez, enrolled as a senior at Exeter High School. Eight months later, Salinas, in his police uniform, was present when Exeter police and Tulare County sheriff's deputies made the bust. They arrested twelve students, ranging in age from fifteen to nineteen, whom Salinas had witnessed and documented selling illegal drugs to other students. Two non-student drug ring members were also arrested. After the bust, Salinas returned to the police department as a patrolman. His career as an undercover agent was short.

Salinas was not a typical narcotics undercover investigator. The job he did, however, was typical of many undercover assignments. His motivations for doing the job were certainly legitimate. He was asked to volunteer for an assignment that would help enforce the drug laws of the state of California. He was also motivated by a desire to "make a difference"— to get harmful drugs out of the schools and off the streets.

Rookie police officer Alex Salinas began his career as an undercover narcotics agent. Posing as high school senior Johnny Ramirez, he helped bust a drug ring operating in two California schools.

Special Agents are for trafficking in drugs in addition to possessing them. The United Nations Office on Drugs and Crime in its *World Drug Report 2010* says, "Drug trafficking is a global illicit trade involving the cultivation, manufacture, distribution and sale of substances which are subject to drug prohibition laws." Federal drug charges for trafficking usually carry longer prison sentences than do those given by states for possession alone.

Drug Laws Are Never Static

Narcotics investigators do not make the laws they enforce. In some cases, they may not even agree with them, but they enforce them nonetheless because they are sworn law enforcement officers. To do their jobs, they have to be very

Marijuana is the most widely used illegal drug in the United States. These bales of marijuana were among the 2 tons (1.8 metric tons) of drugs confiscated in a drug bust in Georgia.

knowledgeable about drug laws. Drugs that are regulated by law are called controlled substances. They are placed into categories called schedules depending on four criteria: whether or not they have acceptable medical uses; whether or not they can be used safely under medical supervision; whether or not a person is likely to become dependent, or get hooked, on them; and whether or not they are drugs that are likely to be abused.

The first drug laws in this country were passed in the late 1800s specifically to control the use of opium in the United States. Since then, drug laws have been passed to deal with the drugs in vogue at the time. For instance, the first drug laws regulating cocaine were passed in 1906, shortly after it was introduced into the United States in soft drinks (Coca-Cola) and patent medicines. New laws regulating cocaine were passed in the 1970s when crack cocaine became readily available. Marijuana was used legally in the United States before the early 1900s, when laws regulating its use first appeared. By 1920, it was the most widely used illegal drug in the United States and remains so today. Lysergic acid diethylamide (LSD) and other hallucinogens came into vogue in the 1960s. In the 1980s, manufactured drugs such as methamphetamines (meth) and ecstasy were very popular. New drug laws followed the development of all of these drugs.

Although marijuana, heroin, cocaine, and meth are still widely used in the United States, prescription drugs used for nonmedical reasons are now the "in" thing. Undercover narcotics investigators are concentrating many of their investigations on pill mills or sham clinics where thousands of prescriptions for medications containing narcotics or other controlled substances are written each year for people who don't really need them. The people who get them then sell them to friends or others who are willing to pay the price. Rogue pharmacies that sell controlled substances with no questions asked are also under investigation by narcotics agents. An article on Consumer.healthday.com says, "There are now more deaths [especially among teens] due to accidental overdoses of prescription painkillers [being used illegally] than due to overdoses of cocaine and heroin combined." The availability of these drugs to young people, who can take them out of their families' unlocked medicine cabinets, contributes to this problem. Richard Miech, a professor of sociology at the University of Colorado in Denver, is quoted in this article as saying, "Most people recognize the dangers of leaving a loaded gun lying around the house. What few people realize is that far more people die as a result of unsecured prescription medications [than from gunshot wounds]."

The illegal use of prescription drugs has recently been eclipsed by the use of synthetic drugs such as "K2" or "Spice" and "bath salts." Spice, which is advertised as a type of herbal incense, consists of plant material that has been laced with chemicals that mimic the effects of tetrahydrocannabinol (THC), the psychoactive ingredient in marijuana. Teens are specifically targeted by people that produce and sell Spice. It is popular with teens because until recently it could be bought

SEIZURES AND SPICE: DEMI'S STORY

On January 29, 2012, a 911 operator received a call for help from a friend of actress Demi Moore. Moore has starred in many movies, including *A Few Good Men* (1992), *GI Jane* (1997), and more recently, *Flawless* (2007) and *Margin Call* (2011). The caller said, "She smoked something—it's not marijuana, but it's similar to incense and [she] seems to be having convulsions of some sort." A story that aired on ABC News 4 in Salt Lake City, Utah, the day after this episode included an interview with Dr. Adam de Havenon, a University of Utah School of Medicine neurologist. Dr. de Havenon began studying the impact of Spice on the brain after two patients that he treated for seizures gave histories of smoking Spice before having their seizures. He said, "These Spice products just seem to activate the seizure area of the brain." Dr. de Havenon also reported that irregularity in heart rhythms and violent behavior were found among Spice users. At the time the story aired, Spice could be purchased cheaply in a variety of stores, as well as over the Internet. The DEA made selling and using Spice illegal in March 2012 by placing it on the controlled substances list.

After a nine-month-long investigation, Oregon narcotic agents seized hundreds of containers of the synthetic marijuana Spice. Three dealers were arrested for selling Spice and other controlled substances.

at a variety of stores, including the corner convenience store. It is also relatively inexpensive. Its use is hard to detect by routine drug screening methods, which is also a positive feature for some teens, especially those involved in sports programs where drug testing is used. It is the second most commonly used drug by high school seniors—second only to marijuana itself. The DEA has now placed it on the controlled substances list because it is highly addictive, has no medical uses, and cannot be used safely even under medical supervision. It can be an extremely dangerous drug to use.

Bath salts contain manmade chemicals related to amphetamines. They can produce hallucinations, suicidal thoughts, violent behavior, extreme paranoia, and a reduced ability to control motor functions such as walking. They are very dangerous to those who use them and to those who may be the recipients of a user's paranoid, violent behavior. They were also placed on the controlled substances list in 2012.

"Making a Difference" Includes Preventing Drug Use

Men and women choose to be narcotics investigators and Special Agents because they believe they can make a difference in the lives of the people they serve by getting drugs off the streets. Narcotics investigators, however, are very realistic. Most doubt that strong enforcement of drug laws *alone* will ever make a significant impact on drug usage in the United States. The use of illegal drugs became so rampant in the 1960s that President Richard Nixon declared a war on drugs in 1971. That war is ongoing. Eugene Jarecki, an independent filmmaker, produced a documentary film in 2012 called *The House I Live In*. It won the Sundance Film Festival's Grand Jury Prize. In the film he claims that over the past forty years, enforcing the war on drugs has cost the United States $1 trillion and has resulted in forty-five million arrests without changing the number of drug abusers in this country.

Realizing the need to do more than battle drug traffickers and others to reduce the supply of drugs, narcotics investigators are expanding their job descriptions. Their new roles are highly visible ones and involve efforts to reduce the demand for drugs. Rich Isaacson has been a DEA Special Agent for more than sixteen years. In an article on GetSmartAboutDrugs.com, SA Isaacson says, "Working for the DEA is very meaningful to me…It is very rewarding to work on drug investigations…but it is not the most rewarding work that I've done in my career. To me, nothing is more important than talking to teenagers and their parents about the dangers of drug use…I try to reduce the demand for illegal drugs through education. Yes, 99 percent of what we do in the DEA is reducing the supply of illegal drugs…Strong enforcement is important, but so is consistent drug [use] prevention."

CHAPTER TWO

HAVING THE RIGHT STUFF

A person invests a lot of time and effort to become a narcotics investigator. Young people need to know if becoming an undercover narcotics investigator is a good career choice for them. They need to know if they have the right stuff to do the job and the likelihood that they will be happy doing it. Before deciding to embark on the lengthy and sometimes dangerous path to this career, young people can do three things that will help them make wise decisions. The first is to take a good, hard, realistic look at themselves. The second is to take a trial run at a law enforcement career by participating in community policing activities that are available to teens. The third is to seek out and enroll in high schools that offer specialized areas of study for future law enforcement officers.

Honest Personal Assessment Is Critical

John Douglas, a well-known and highly respected Federal Bureau of Investigation (FBI) Special Agent, turned to writing and teaching after twenty-five years with the FBI. In his book, *John Douglas's Guide to Landing a Career in Law Enforcement*, Special Agent Douglas says that self-assessment is critical before a person considers a law enforcement career of any type. Law enforcement is not a career that one should choose because it appears to be glamorous on television and in the movies. It is not a career that one should undertake just because a best friend, a father, a grandfather, or a personal hero is a law enforcement officer. Special Agent Douglas says, "The truth [about one's self] should be the starting point for a law enforcement career." Four questions people should seek to answer in their self-evaluations are:

- What am I really good at doing?
- What things do I really enjoy doing? What things do I hate to do?
- What situations make me extremely uncomfortable, nervous, or anxious?
- Am I a confident, strong person?

A person who enjoys working with groups of people is more likely to succeed and be happy in a law enforcement career than is a person who prefers to work entirely alone. A person who gets extremely anxious when confronted by anger or hostility won't be happy in any law enforcement career. On the other hand, a person with strong self-esteem who can mold his or her strengths into a leadership role will be very happy in law enforcement. He or she will

Law enforcement officers must enjoy and be good at working with others to be successful and happy in the profession. The ability to work with teens is essential.

make an excellent narcotics investigator.

In his book, Special Agent Douglas discusses what he calls "intangible traits" that most successful law enforcement officers have. These are values that most people are taught from an early age. Five of these traits are:

- Tolerance. The United States is truly a melting pot in which people of many races, religions, and beliefs have been blended to form a unique society. A successful law enforcement officer must be tolerant or accepting of diversity among the people with whom he or she will work.
- Empathy. A popular phrase that describes empathy is "being

EXPLORER CADET RAISES MONEY FOR FAMILIES OF FALLEN OFFICERS

Jennifer Rubin is a fifteen-year-old member of the Chesterfield, Missouri, Police Department Explorer Post 9270. In 2012 she attended the National Law Enforcement Exploring Conference in Ft. Collins, Colorado. A newsletter, *BOLO*, which was generated at the conference, featured an article about Jennifer. When she was in the fifth grade, Jennifer realized that the law enforcement officers in her community were special people. They devoted their lives to protecting the citizens of St. Louis, Missouri, and East St. Louis, Illinois, and occasionally lost their lives in the line of duty. At age twelve, Jennifer started a fund-raising project called Rockin'4Relief to raise money to provide assistance for families of law enforcement officers in her community who had been killed. Initially she received pledges and donations totaling over $700 for rocking in a rocking chair for ten hours in her local high school gymnasium. She then took her rocking chair to a local grocery store and tripled her take. In 2011, she asked her fellow explorers for help. They raised nearly $10,000 by Rockin' in seven locations in their

community. Shortly before going to the conference in Colorado, Jennifer received a call from TV celebrity Oprah Winfrey, who donated $13,000 to Jennifer's fund-raising efforts. With continued help from Law Enforcement Explorers across the country, Jennifer hopes to "help law enforcement families nationwide."

able to walk in another person's shoes." Empathy is the ability to share in another's emotions, thoughts, or feelings. Successful law enforcement officers must be empathetic to those with whom they work and for whom they work.

- Flexibility. "Rolling with the punches" is a slang way to describe flexibility. Successful law enforcement officers can't be rigid. They must be able to make day-to-day changes to accommodate the many situations that they encounter in their jobs. This is especially necessary for undercover narcotics investigators whose lives may depend on their flexibility.

- Respect. Like the military, law enforcement organizations are hierarchical. Police officers are accountable to detectives, detectives to sergeants, and on up the ranks. To work successfully within the system, police officers must respect authority. They must accept decisions and directions from those above them in rank.

- Integrity. Being honest and incorruptible are traits that all law enforcement officers must have. Undercover narcotics investigators can be tempted by the drugs and money that surround them. A person's deep-seated integrity is his or her safeguard against these temptations.

Having these five traits is a must for law enforcement officers and is of benefit in any career a person may choose.

Important Skills to Develop

Paul Bagley, a retired police officer, on Netplace.com, says that young people can develop skills that will enhance their chances of being accepted into law enforcement academies and/or jobs. The first two skills that Bagley mentions go hand in hand—interpersonal skills and communication skills. When one skill is improved, the other also improves. One

Students with good communication skills have a "leg up" when applying for law enforcement academies. This student is enhancing his ability to communicate by taking a public speaking course.

of the most important things one can do to improve interpersonal and communication skills is to learn to listen carefully to what others have to say. Young people should also learn to choose words carefully so that the messages they are trying to convey are absolutely clear to listeners. People with good interpersonal and communication skills are assertive. They learn to express their feelings in ways that others can understand and respect without feeling threatened.

Author Charles Sipes interviewed Gary Killam, president of the Florida Gang Investigation Association, for an article entitled "Advice for Becoming a Gang Investigator." In the interview, Killam said, "One of

Being adept at the use of computers is a skill that is extremely valuable in law enforcement. People with computer skills have an advantage when applying to law enforcement academies.

the biggest skills I see lacking in young people wanting to get into law enforcement are communication skills. If you are going to get into the field of law enforcement, you need to talk to anyone, anytime, at any place. I see young officers coming in who are uncomfortable talking to people and this is a people business. You have to have great communication skills..."

Having a gift for languages is a big plus for law enforcement officers. Bagley says that fewer than 10 percent of law enforcement officers in the United States are fluent in a language other than English. Those who are fluent in other languages have huge advantages when being considered for police academies or DEA positions. The languages that are most helpful for law enforcement officers in the United States are Spanish, French, Portuguese, Arabic, Italian, Chinese, and Korean. Most high schools and many middle schools offer elective courses in foreign languages. Being fluent in a second language will be beneficial to young people regardless of what careers they choose.

Bagley suggests that all students interested in law enforcement consider taking speech courses or participating on debate teams to enhance their abilities to speak in public. Attaining acting skills will also be helpful, especially for undercover agents. People who get experience in broadcasting while enhancing their speaking and acting skills will have valuable credentials for law enforcement jobs. Being adept in the use of computers, audio and video recording devices, and cameras also enhances the credentials of a person applying for law enforcement academies or jobs.

High School Opportunities in Policing

To help young people decide whether law enforcement careers are of interest to them, police and sheriff's departments, the DEA, and other federal agencies have developed programs for high school students to give them hands-on experience in policing. One such program is Law Enforcement Career Exploring (LECE). Some police departments have also joined with educational institutions to develop Police Academy Magnet Schools.

Law Enforcement Career Exploring originated when the Boy Scouts of America (BSA) developed special explorer posts for teenage boys who were interested in law enforcement. Today, LECE offers all teens the opportunity to gain exposure to various criminal justice careers. It also allows them to have positive interactions with law enforcement professionals. Teens who are involved in LECE improve their abilities to work with others because teamwork is a key element of the program. Explorers are challenged to improve their physical and mental fitness, their self-discipline, and their personal conduct. They work with law enforcement personnel in specific activities that are not only instructive to

Law Enforcement Career Exploring teaches self-discipline, self-confidence, self-respect, and teamwork. These Explorers put teamwork to practical use in a game of tug-of-war.

themselves but also are of benefit to the communities in which they live.

The Philadelphia Police Department in Pennsylvania sponsors an Explorer program that is typical of other such programs. Philadelphia Police Explorers belong to Explorer Post 991. They range in age from fourteen to twenty and spend every Saturday working with fellow Explorers at the Philadelphia Police Academy. The goal of the program, as listed on PPDexplorers.org, is to teach young adults the values needed to succeed in a law enforcement careers and in life. These values include self-discipline, self-confidence, self-respect, and team-work. Explorers are trained in many skills, including firearms safety and use, first aid, crime scene searches, crowd and traffic control, accident investigation, and controlled substance awareness. Students who are sophomores and juniors in high school receive a chance to attend the State Police Youth Week in York, Pennsylvania. It is a six-day camp used to introduce Explorers to procedures of law enforcement. They also go on Law Enforcement Training and Education tours in Washington, D.C. This program provides hands-on-training, lectures, and tours conducted by the Washington, D.C., Metropolitan Police, the U.S. Park Police, the U.S. Capitol Police, the U.S. Secret Service, the DEA, the FBI, and other federal agencies. Some Post 991 Explorers also attend the Fort Indiantown Gap Summer Boot Camp Training program at the Fort Indiantown Gap Military Base. The emphasis of this program is intensive physical fitness training.

Many communities in the United States have Police Academy Magnet Schools for students who express an interest in careers in law enforcement. Perhaps the most extensive law enforcement magnet school program is in the Los Angeles, California, school system. The Los Angeles Police Academy magnet school curriculum goes beyond basic high school course requirements. It provides students with specialized coursework, training, mentoring, work, and volunteer opportunities. There are five high schools in the Los Angeles area with this program. More than five hundred students are involved. In addition to the regular high school curriculum, the program includes instruction in the following areas:

- Communication skills emphasizing listening, reading, speaking, writing, and thinking as it relates to law enforcement.
- Basic concepts of criminal law, principles of law enforcement, constitutional law, the criminal justice system, and other law-related topics.
- Health training, including mental and physical health.
- The role of science and technology in solving crimes.
- Computer science as it relates to law enforcement.

Other magnet schools include the Sandra Day O'Connor Criminal Justice/Public Service Academy (CSPSA) in Austin High School, El Paso, Texas, and the Judge Barefoot Sanders Law Magnet in Dallas, Texas. The goals of these schools are similar to that of the Los Angeles Police Academy magnet schools.

CHAPTER THREE

BECOMING AN UNDERCOVER NARCOTICS INVESTIGATOR

The process of becoming an undercover narcotics investigator is a lengthy one. It may take six or more years from the time candidates first apply for employment in law enforcement agencies until they find themselves working undercover to bust drug rings. The first step in reaching the goal is to complete the application for a position in a law enforcement agency. Once the job has been secured, the second step is to acquire the training necessary to do the job. The third step is to get hands-on experience in many aspects of policing while taking every opportunity to acquire the skills needed by narcotics investigators.

Applying for a Job in Law Enforcement

Applicants for law enforcement jobs must meet the following basic requirements:

- They must be citizens or naturalized citizens of the United States.
- They must be twenty-one years old by the time of employment.
- They must be high school graduates or have General Educational Development (GED) certificates. Most law enforcement agencies are now requiring candidates for employment to have associate's degrees from accredited colleges, at least

The Los Angeles Police Department (LAPD) actively seeks recruits for its police academy at career fairs throughout California. Positions at the academy are highly prized.

sixty to ninety hours of college credits, or three to five years of military service.

- They must have valid driver's licenses and good driving records with no convictions for driving while intoxicated (DWI).
- They must have no criminal convictions and no history of criminal activity or improper conduct.
- They must have good employment records and no irresponsible financial histories.
- They must have an honorable discharge if applying after serving in the military.
- They must have no history of illegal drug use. This

Law enforcement academy training emphasizes physical fitness. Recruits at the New Jersey State Police Academy, shown here, complete the running portion of their physical qualification examination.

requirement is no longer an absolute disqualifier in most police departments. Applicants who have used marijuana in the past, but who no longer use it, are evaluated on an individual basis rather than being disqualified immediately. A history of the use of other illegal drugs is usually considered a disqualifier as is current use of any illegal drug.

- They must be of good moral character with an abundance of personal integrity.

Candidates who meet all of these requirements are eligible to take entry-level law enforcement written examinations. Many local and state police departments have Web sites that include study guides for their written examinations.

In addition to the written examination, applicants must take a physical abilities test. This test varies among law enforcement agencies but usually involves testing an applicant's ability to do a particular number of sit-ups and push-ups within a certain time limit. It may also require the applicant to run a specific distance in a specific amount of time or to be able to lift a designated amount of weight. Men applying to the police academy in Vermont, for instance, must be able to bench-press weights as heavy as 99 percent of their body weights, and complete thirty-eight sit-ups in one minute and twenty-nine push-ups in a minute. Women applicants must be able to bench-press 59 percent of their body weights, and complete thirty-two sit-ups in a minute and fifteen push-ups in a minute. The state of Arkansas has similar push-up and sit-up requirements but adds the ability to do a 14-inch (35.6-centimeter) vertical jump and run 328 yards (300 meters) in 1.3 minutes.

Applicants who successfully complete the written and physical abilities tests must then undergo an oral board interview. Dr. Richard Weinblatt in an article on Policelink .monster.com reports that the oral boards are the key to getting hired. He gives ten tips to increase an applicant's chance of making a good impression on board members. Some of his suggestions include being early for the interview and being appropriately dressed and groomed. He especially recommends removing all nose rings, tongue piercings, and earrings; making eye contact with interviewers; sounding confident; and thanking and shaking hands with all board members at the end of the interview. The number of Web sites and books written for those preparing for oral interviews supports the importance of this portion of the application process.

An applicant who successfully completes the oral board interview then undergoes an extensive background check, is fingerprinted, and has a comprehensive physical examination, including an eye examination. Applicants must have 20/20 vision in one eye and at least 20/40 vision in the other eye. If their visual acuity isn't that good, it must be correctable to that level with glasses or contact lenses. In the United States, 20/20 vision is considered to be normal (in the metric system, the standard is six meters and it's called 6/6 vision). An evaluation by a psychologist and a polygraph test

THE NATIONAL POLICE OFFICER SELECTION TEST (POST) IS USED BY MANY AGENCIES

Stanard and Associates, Inc., is a human resources consulting firm that specializes in employee testing and assessment systems. It has developed **POST**, the exam given to entry-level employees by more than one thousand law enforcement agencies across the United States. The exam has four sections. The first measures a person's ability to add, subtract, multiply, divide, determine percentages, and calculate averages. An example of a question from this section of the examination, given on USCapitolPolice.gov, is:

During one 5-day period, Officer Fernandez drove his patrol motorcycle 225 miles. If he drove 85 miles on one day, how many miles did he average on each of the other days?

A. 28 miles
B. 35 miles
C. 40 miles
D. 70 miles
E. 140 miles

[Answer: B]

The second section tests reading comprehension, whereas the third section measures a person's ability to spell and use grammar and punctuation correctly. The last section measures a person's ability to write complete sentences with correct spelling, grammar, and punctuation. Agencies that use **POST** have study guides provided by Stanard and Associates that are available to those taking the examination.

complete the application process. Those that successfully complete this battery of tests are ready for employment or training in a police academy.

Obtaining Training in Police Academies

Almost all law enforcement officers get their basic police training in police academies. Many law enforcement candidates pay for their own training before being hired by law enforcement agencies. The Cedar Valley College Law Enforcement Academy in Lancaster, Texas, is a police academy that is directly affiliated with a college. Students enrolling in this academy pay college tuition. They purchase their own uniforms, books, handcuffs, batons, and duty belts. They also pay ammunition and shooting range fees. The basic Peace Officer course at this academy consists of 720 hours of study in thirty-four subjects. Graduates of the program receive associate's degrees and are eligible to take the Texas Police Officer Exam. They then apply for jobs. When they are hired, they may be reimbursed for part or all of their educational expenses by the hiring agency.

Perhaps the most famous and prestigious of all police academies is the Los Angeles Police Department (LAPD) Academy. Applicants who

Recruits for the Chicago Police Academy (CPA) are pictured here at a flag-raising ceremony honoring fallen officers. In 2012, 450 recruits were chosen for six months of intensive training at CPA.

are selected for jobs with the LAPD are sent to the academy for six months of training. The training is free and officers are paid their full starting salaries during training. The academy curriculum includes basic academic subjects such as arrest and booking procedures and report writing. Cadets are also taught defensive driving and vehicular pursuit techniques with an emphasis on vehicular safety. Firearms training includes weapon care and safety and marksmanship, among other skills. Cultural sensitivity training, stress management, and techniques for dealing with domestic violence are among the topics covered in human relations courses. Laws covering many areas of policing are

Vehicular pursuit and stop techniques are taught at police academies and at the DEA Academy. DEA trainees are shown here completing a mock vehicular stop.

also presented, as are tactical courses that help officers to deal with building searches, crimes in progress, the use of deadly force, and many other situations that may arise. A significant amount of time at the academy is spent in physical training. At the end of the six months of training, cadets are in excellent physical condition. They have also learned many self-defense techniques that will be useful in their careers.

A Leg Up on the Competition

Getting a job in a law enforcement agency is challenging. The competition for the few positions that are available is fierce. Police academy appointments may also be difficult to get. There are two strategies that will improve a person's chances of getting the law enforcement job or the police academy appointment that he or she wants. The first is to have a college degree before applying for a position. The second is to apply to a police cadet program.

Almost without exception, a person must have at least sixty hours of college credit to be considered for even the smallest of police forces. Most state police jobs require a candidate to have a four-year college degree. An associate of science (AS) law enforcement degree is designed for students who hope to be law enforcement officers. It can usually be obtained within two years and is frequently offered at community colleges, vocational-technical schools, and four-year colleges. These courses combine practical training in police procedures with courses that cover topics such as

NYPD CADET CORPS MEMBERS EARN WHILE THEY LEARN

The New York Police Department (NYPD) Cadet Corps is an apprenticeship program that benefits both members of the corps and the NYPD. Cadets work full-time during summer months and part-time during the school year while they attend college. They receive $10,000 of college tuition assistance annually. A cadet who becomes a police officer in the NYPD and works for two years does not have to repay the money he or she received for tuition assistance. Besides tuition assistance, cadets receive a competitive hourly wage, paid sick leave, and paid vacations. They receive hands-on experience in community policing and problem solving. They are also trained in many of the topics and techniques that are taught at police academies. When they reach the age of twenty-one, cadets can apply for police academy training and jobs with the NYPD. The benefit of this program to the NYPD is that it has a large pool of experienced candidates from which to hire new recruits. In June 2011, sixty-six police cadets graduated from the corps. All went on to the NYPD Police Academy. At that time, there were 1,827 former Corps Cadets working for the NYPD.

criminology, criminal justice ethics, crime scene investigation, report writing, community policing, and police management.

There are many courses in criminal justice available on the Internet. A person taking an online course must be very disciplined, be a self-starter, and have good computer skills. If the courses taken are from a nationally accredited college, they can be of significant value to a person applying for a law enforcement academy position or a law enforcement job.

Police cadet programs are available in many large cities in the United States. Cadet Corps are law enforcement apprenticeship programs that offer training to young people between the ages of eighteen and twenty-one. The programs give qualified men and women a chance to experience the challenges and personal rewards of a police career before they are old enough to apply for police academy training.

Additional Training for Narcotics Investigators

Most narcotics investigators have been promoted to the rank of detective or higher before they are assigned to investigator positions. In the three years or so that it takes to get the assignment, police officers take special training courses to acquire the knowledge and the skills to do narcotics investigation. They also take additional college courses leading to bachelor's degrees in criminology, criminal justice, psychology, or related fields.

Regional DEA offices provide special training courses for state and local narcotic agents. The DEA Basic Narcotics Investigator's Course is two weeks long and is intended for police officers who are new to drug law enforcement. Attendees are given current and relevant information on a variety of topics, including officer survival, drug identification, surveillance techniques, informant management, and undercover techniques. The DEA Advanced Narcotics Investigator's Course is four to five days long and is intended for drug law enforcement officers who have at least two years of experience.

The International Association of Undercover Officers offers a variety of educational opportunities for narcotics investigators to hone their skills in undercover work. The Institute of Police Technology and Management of the University of North Florida and Pathfinders Consultants International, a firm of private investigators, are two other agencies that offer special training for undercover investigators. All of the courses offered by these agencies improve the chances that undercover narcotics investigators will be successful and safe in their fight against those who deal in illegal drugs.

CHAPTER FOUR

DEA SPECIAL AGENTS: FEDERAL NARCOTICS INVESTIGATORS

Areport from the U.S. Department of Justice on justice.gov/dea/careers says that DEA Special Agents are a very select group of men and women. "They come from a variety of backgrounds and play a vital and exclusive role in combating the critical problems of drug trafficking by taking on exciting and significant challenges." Special Agents are the backbone of the DEA. They are the men and women whose job, according to information from the DEA itself, is "to bring to justice organizations—including those with ties to terrorism—and their principal members who are involved in the growing, manufacture, and distribution of controlled substances." There are more than 5,000 DEA Special Agents working in 226 cities within the United States and in 85 offices in 65 countries around the globe. Working as an undercover DEA Special Agent abroad can be very exciting, but it is one of the most dangerous jobs in all of law enforcement.

Getting Ahead of the Competition

The competition for SA positions with the DEA has always been intense. Writer Adam Stone, in an article on MilitaryTimesEdge .com, reports that in July 2008, the DEA had eight thousand applications for two hundred Special Agent positions. In February 2010, there were twelve thousand applicants for the two hundred Special Agent slots. Applicants who are not chosen in a particular hiring "window" frequently return to school to enhance their credentials or seek jobs in other compatible occupations in hopes they will be chosen for the DEA in the future.

DEA agents pictured in this training exercise are among 5,000 agents who work in 226 cities within the United States and in 65 countries around the world.

One way of getting an edge on the competition is to participate in a government internship program while in high

school or college. An article from the
federal government's Office of Personnel
Management says that internships are
"designed to provide students enrolled in a
wide variety of educational institutions
from high school to graduate level with
opportunities to work in agencies and
explore Federal careers while still in
school and while getting paid for the work
performed." Manny Thompson, a senior at
Wichita State University in Wichita,
Kansas, who is majoring in criminal justice, is featured in an article on Wichita
.edu. He is a DEA intern through the
university's Cooperative Education and
Work-Based Learning Program. He does
clerical work in the DEA field office but
also works with DEA agents as they participate in joint operations with members
of the Wichita Police Department, the
Kansas Highway Patrol, and the Kansas
Bureau of Investigation.

Ferris State University's Henry
Snowden Jr. is a summer intern at the
Saginaw, Michigan, DEA field office. In an
article on Ferris's Web site, Snowden reports that through
his internship he has developed an understanding of how
drug dealers operate and how DEA agents execute their

Michele Leonhart speaks at the 2010 International Drug Enforcement Conference in Rio de Janeiro, Brazil. Eight months later she became the first female administrator of the DEA.

mission when it comes to catching drug dealers. Besides filing and shredding documents, Snowden rides along with agents and participates in surveillance of suspected drug dealers. He says, "I am getting a lot of hands-on experience

DEA SPECIAL AGENT RECEIVES AWARD FOR EXCEPTIONAL HEROISM

DEA Special Agent Timothy Sellers is one of the first to agree that the life of a DEA agent can be exciting and is often very, very dangerous. In the acknowledgment page of his recently published book, *The Last Cowboy: The True Story of One of DEA's Most Decorated Undercover Agents*, SA Sellers speaks of one of his motivations for becoming a DEA agent. He had "youthful dreams of riding the badlands with John Wayne, thumping black-hatted Bad Barts, or today's equivalent, the sleazy drug traffickers and terror dudes that make the good citizens silent." In one of Sellers's last assignments before his retirement from the DEA, he took the opportunity to give a major thump to several Bad Barts—fourteen Hizb-i-Islami Gulbuddin and Taliban terrorists. A biographical sketch of Sellers on LastCowboy.com tells how he prevented a planned attack on U.S. and NATO forces and saved the lives of many Afghan citizens. He tackled an armed suicide bomber as he was boarding a bus loaded with innocent Afghans, just blocks from U.S. and NATO military headquarters, the Presidential Palace, and

the American Embassy. The bomber and thir-
teen other members of his terrorist cell were
arrested. Special Agent Sellers and a U.S.
Embassy attaché, Jeffery Higgins, who was with
Sellers when he tackled the terrorist, received
the 2005 U.S. Attorney General's Award for
Exceptional Heroism for "extraordinary acts of
courage and voluntary risk of life during the
performance of official duties."

from each agent, and it has been a great way to network inside the federal government."

Students who are really interested in being DEA Special Agents can also get an edge on their competitors by developing specific skills while in high school and college. The DEA is particularly interested in hiring people who are fluent in other languages. Fluency in Spanish, French, Russian, Hebrew, Chinese Mandarin, Farsi, Urdu, dialects of Nigerian languages, or any Balkan language will be very helpful for an applicant. The DEA also looks for applicants who are pilots or who have worked as ship's officers or navigators. Being especially skilled in the use of computers and other electronic gear is also very helpful.

Although guys might think it's reverse discrimination, qualified young women may have an edge over their male counterparts in securing positions as DEA Special Agents at the present time. Only about 9 percent of current Special Agents are women, and the DEA would like to have more.

Applying for a DEA Special Agent Position

Completing the application process for SA positions takes at least a year. Before starting, the DEA recommends that applicants take the eligibility quiz, which is found on its Web site. The quiz includes questions about a person's health and physical conditioning, as well as his or her educational and life experiences. The results of this quiz are available almost immediately. The quiz is meant to weed out people with physical limitations such as poor eyesight or hearing and those who are not college graduates or who have none of the skills that the DEA is seeking in its Special Agents. If a person passes the eligibility quiz and wishes to pursue a career as an SA, applicants are encouraged to attend one of the Special Agent Applicant Orientation sessions given at DEA field offices across the country. The location of the offices and the name of the recruitment coordinator for each office are listed on the DEA Web site, http://www.justice.gov/dea.

There are nine parts to the DEA hiring process. They are almost exactly the same as those previously described for people applying for positions as local and state law enforcement officers. They include the pre-application quiz, a review of qualifications, a written examination, a physical task test (PTT), an oral panel interview, a medical examination, a psychological assessment, a polygraph examination, and a full background check. Requirements in addition to those needed for positions in other agencies include the following:

- Possession of at least a bachelor's degree with a grade point average of 2.95 or higher. Some military experience may be substituted for a bachelor's degree, especially if the applicant is a pilot, a ship's officer, or an accountant, or is fluent in a foreign language.
- Being willing to relocate anywhere in the United States or to foreign posts.
- Being qualified for top-secret security clearance.
- Being no older than thirty-six years of age. Unlike other law enforcement agencies, the DEA does not accept applicants who are older than thirty-six. It also has a mandatory retirement age of fifty-seven.

The physical task test that DEA applicants must pass is also somewhat more rigorous than the physical ability tests of other law enforcement agencies. It requires applicants to make at least a minimum score doing pull-ups, sit-ups, and push-ups. It also requires applicants to complete a "shuttle run" as quickly as possible. In a shuttle run, a person runs 30 yards (27.4 m) around a series of obstacles. The run is meant to show a person's agility. The PTT concludes with a 2-mile (3.2 km) run. Minimum scores for successful completion of the PTT vary with the applicant's age and gender. A

WOMEN DEA AGENTS: FEW BUT MIGHTY

The **DEA Museum** in **Arlington, Virginia**, contains a fascinating history of the **DEA**, including the roles that women have and continue to play in the agency. In 1933, **Elizabeth Bass**, a longtime friend of First Lady **Eleanor Roosevelt**, became the first female federal narcotics investigator. She later became the district supervisor of narcotics agents in **Chicago, Illinois**. **Mary Turner** was the first female graduate of the **DEA's** Special Agent training program. She graduated first in her class in 1973. A year later, there were twenty-three female Special Agents working in **DEA** field offices throughout the United States. Today, there are 450 female Special Agents. That number is only 9 percent of the five thousand **DEA** Special Agents.

They may not be numerous, but several female Special Agents hold high positions in the agency. **Pam Brown** was Supervisory Special Agent for Southeast Asia, based in **Chiang Mai, Thailand**, until being transferred to **Washington, D.C.**, in 2010. She had been a **DEA** agent for twenty-one years when she received the assignment in Thailand. **Barbara Roach** became the

Special Agent in Charge (SAC) of the Denver, Colorado, field office in January 2012. She is responsible for overseeing DEA activities in Colorado, Utah, Wyoming, and Montana. She has been a Special Agent for twenty-five years. And then there is Michele Leonhart, who has served the DEA for the last thirty-two years. On December 22, 2010, she became the administrator of the DEA. She directs the $3 billion agency and is responsible for more than ten thousand employees in domestic offices throughout the United States and in sixty-seven foreign countries.

Today there are 450 women, one of whom is pictured here, among the 5,000 DEA Special Agents working around the world.

the use of automated information systems. Trainees are introduced to the skills they will need when working undercover. These include working with informants, surveillance techniques, role-playing, and other talents that new agents will perfect in more advanced training programs and while working with experienced agents. The rigorous physical fitness and defensive tactics programs provided to trainees are conducted at the FBI Academy, which is adjacent to the DEA Academy. At least 122 hours of firearms training is included, as are driving courses, self-defense courses, and courses in how to conduct proper arrests and serve search warrants.

Successful completion of basic training requires a candidate to maintain an 80

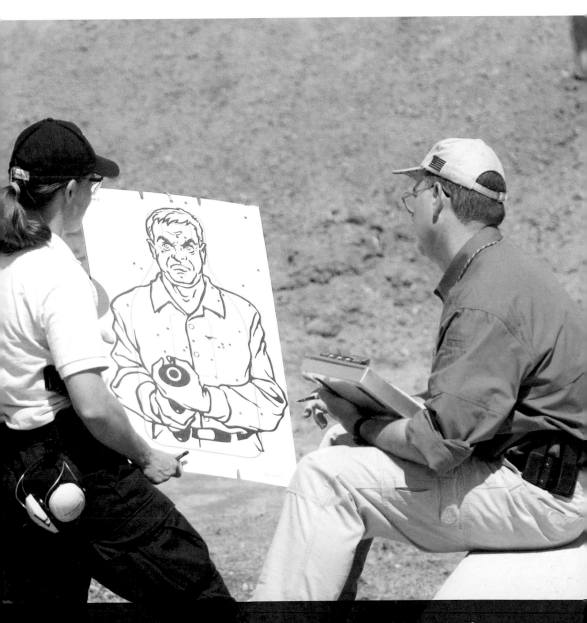

DEA Special Agent training requires candidates to successfully complete firearms qualification tests. Trainees, shown here at the DEA Academy firing range, discuss shot placement with an instructor.

percent average on all exams, pass the firearms qualification test, pass rigorous physical task tests, and successfully demonstrate leadership and sound decision-making qualities. After graduation from the DEA Academy, rookie agents are assigned to field offices, where they continue to learn, mentored by more senior agents. The DEA Academy also offers an extensive number of courses that agents take throughout their careers. For instance, agents must attend Advanced Agent Training School between their second and fifth years of employment. This one-week course places emphasis on tactical training, handling informants, electronic surveillance techniques, and other skills that were introduced in basic training. These skills are critical if agents are to work safely in undercover situations. This course must be completed before agents begin to work as undercover investigators.

CHAPTER FIVE

THE SPECIFICS OF UNDERCOVER WORK

"Ahhhhhh, the life of a narcotics officer. It is just like the movies, drinking champagne, cruising in your custom Denali, screaming down the water in your 'Go Fast' cigar boat, and sitting in a hot tub with a hand-rolled Cuban [cigar]...Yes, unfortunately, this still appears to be the image of the undercover narcotics agent, and somehow the foundation or 'motivation' for many young officers to make their way into the narcotics world." Darin Logue, who wrote these words for an article on Officer .com, is a consultant and part-time agent for a major Midwest narcotics task force. He suggests that the only legitimate motivation for pursuing a career as a narcotics investigator is to work with a team of people, all of whom are dedicated to making a positive difference in society. He calls undercover work "American policing at its best." Logue goes on to say that choosing the right people for narcotics investigator positions, all of whom should be volunteers, is the most important aspect of good undercover work. These people must then be thoroughly trained for the job.

Narcotics investigators develop many skills. Among them is the ability to safely deal with the cleanup of meth labs and other places where illegal drugs are manufactured.

Police officers and DEA agents who complete the three or more years of training to become narcotics investigators have the right stuff for the job. By seeking these jobs, they have volunteered to work undercover if necessary. They are proficient in developing operational plans, they know the ins and outs of working with informants, and they have mastered the surveillance equipment that they will need to do their jobs. Many of them are good enough at role-playing that they could star in movies. Safely dealing with meth labs and other places where illegal drugs are manufactured is among their many skills. They are also knowledgeable about the legal aspects of undercover work. Walking the fine line between what is legal and what is not becomes a way of life.

Developing Operational Plans

Undercover investigators are rarely the lone wolves portrayed in popular television shows and in the movies. A successful under-cover investigation is a team effort. Thomas Burton, a twenty-five-year veteran of the DEA, is now a law enforce-ment trainer and consultant. In "Undercover Officer Safety," he says, "Undercover operations should always be well thought out, planned and prepared...The importance of an operational plan cannot be overstated. It keeps investigators focused on what they are doing and reduces dangerous unplanned changes to the operation." These plans identify who the drug dealers are. They also identify the specific members of the team: the undercover agent(s), the case control officer (street supervisor), surveillance team mem-bers, the office supervisor, and others. The plans also designate when and where operations will take place and what the objectives of each step of the operations are. It is imperative that *everyone*, from undercover agents them-selves to radio operators know exactly what the plan involves and have written copies of it. To be productive and safe, the operation must then be carried out as planned.

The Role of Surveillance in Undercover Work

Dick Tracy, a comic-strip detective, had his radio wristwatch. James Bond (007) had his fountain pen camera. Undercover agents today have their own very sophisticated surveillance toys to play with. Brian Baker and Whitney Gunter, in an article on ifpo.org, say, "Surveillance is a game of watching others without being noticed and a game of gathering information without appearing to care." In actuality, surveillance is far from a game. It is the key to a successful undercover operation. Undercover operations are all about gathering hard evidence against drug dealers, and there are many sophisticated pieces of equipment to help do the job.

There is an old adage that says, "A picture is worth a thousand words." Photographs or videos of drug dealers caught in the act of selling drugs to undercover agents are very hard pieces of evidence in trials against drug dealers. Far from 007's fountain pen camera, today's sophisticated cameras are small enough to be easily concealed. They can see in the dark or from drone aircraft flying high over the borders where drugs are smuggled into the United States. Pictures that they take can be downloaded into computers almost instantaneously or can be watched in real time.

Second only to pictures, recordings of drug deals going down are also evidence that can be used against drug dealers. Telephones can be bugged to gather this evidence. Cell phones, especially those that contain a global positioning system (GPS) can be used to locate drug dealers and to follow them. Cell phone conversations can also be monitored, as can e-mail messages and text messages. Although it is risky to do it, undercover agents may wear wires to record conversations that can later be used at trials.

Camera-carrying drone aircraft, similar to the one being launched by this soldier in Afghanistan, are among the surveillance tools used by DEA Special Agents worldwide.

Cameras and audio surveillance devices are just a few of the tools used by undercover narcotics investigators. Investigators that are especially adept in the use of surveillance devices are in big demand by all law enforcement agencies. Just knowing how to use the equipment, however, is not enough. Narcotics investigators must also know how to use them legally. Surveillance should never be undertaken without permission to do so by a legal authority. There are many laws that apply to the various surveillance techniques mentioned. If these techniques are used without getting judicial approval to do so, the information gathered may not be admissible in court. In the extreme, unauthorized

FILMMAKER GOES BIONIC

Canadian Rob Spence is a documentary film-maker who is presently working on a movie describing the global spread of the use of surveillance cameras. He sustained an injury to his right eye as a child that eventually necessitated that the eye be removed and replaced with a prosthetic eye. One day, while looking at the camera in his cell phone, he realized that the camera was small enough to fit into his artificial eye. He could use the concealed camera to become a human surveillance machine while interviewing people for his documentary. Holly Fox, in an article written for MSNBC.MSN.com, says that Spence has had help from several engineers in developing this device. Among them is Steve Mann, cofounder of the wearable computer research group at Massachusetts Institute of Technology in Cambridge, Massachusetts. The camera was provided by OmniVision, Inc., a company based in Santa Clara, California. Executives of the company hope that success with the eye camera will speed up research already underway to restore vision to blind people.

> **Fox says that Spence acknowledges privacy concerns. He says, "The closer I get to putting this camera eye in, the more freaked out people are about me. People aren't sure they want to hang around someone who might be filming them at any time."**

surveillance may become the grounds for legal action against law enforcement agencies.

Working with Confidential Informants

An article from the American Civil Liberties Union, an organization dedicated to protecting the constitutional rights of all citizens of the United States, notes, "Unlike witnesses, informants are motivated by self-advancement. Informants work for the government, often secretly, to gather and provide information or to testify in exchange for cash or leniency in punishment for their own crimes. Preliminary research indicates that up to 80 percent of all drug cases in America may be based on information provided by informants. An informant can be a useful law enforcement tool...if used properly."

Brian Lieberman, supervisor of special investigations of the Winter Haven Police Department in Florida, agrees that using information from informants can be risky. He says, "Informants are often criminals themselves; if not properly

Narcotics agents from a meth task force are shown questioning a confidential informant before busting a crystal meth manufacturing lab in California's Central Valley, the meth capital of America.

managed, they can render a law enforcement investigation useless, destroy an agency's credibility, and even endanger officers' lives." If undercover narcotics investigators want to use information from an informant, they must establish the informant's credibility and reliability. Has the informant provided information in previous operations that proved to be reliable? Is the informant in a position within a drug cartel or a gang to have access to accurate and useful information? These are only two of the questions that agents must be able to answer. Information received from informants must be double-checked before being believed.

Just as agents should have judicial approval

before undertaking surveillance operations, they also need supervisory or judicial approval before making deals with informants. Agents need to make sure that informants clearly understand the conditions of the agreement with the law enforcement agency. Agents should never make promises to informants that they do not have the authority to keep.

Role-Playing in Undercover Work

One of the most important and necessary talents an undercover agent can have is the ability to role-play. In her book *Art of Darkness: Ingenious Performances by Undercover Operators, Con Men and Others*, Sara Schneider, an anthropologist who has a background in human performance studies, offers many suggestions to help agents work successfully and safely. Author Charles Remsberg summarizes the suggestions in an article on PoliceOne.com. Three of the suggestions are the following:

- Build the right truths into cover stories. Dr. Schneider says, "How elaborate your false identity has to be depends on the degree of distrust you're likely to encounter. If you're after people who are openly and carelessly selling drugs, your undercover persona can be very light. But for some very complicated investigations, you may have to essentially create another life." She stresses the importance of using the K.I.S.S. principle [keep it simple, stupid].

- Believe in oneself in the role. Dr. Schneider says, "Your assumed role has to be so well embedded in your mind and memory that you virtually believe it yourself."

- Develop your gift for gab—and silence. The best undercover agents can talk the talk of their suspects. They can keep a conversation going regardless of its content or where it's being held. Knowing when to remain silent is also a must. Dr. Schneider quotes a famous FBI undercover agent, Sal Vizzini, who said, "I had to remind myself above all to shut up. One of the hardest cons is saying nothing at all...If you want to give the impression of being cool, the less you say the better."

Drug Labs and Hydroponic Marijuana Farming

Clandestine drug laboratories, commonly called "clan labs," manufacture many types of illegal drugs. Probably the most common and dangerous of these are meth labs. Glenn Ketcham and Vince McLeod are industrial hygienists who write about the dangers of clan labs. Because of the chemicals used to make drugs and the wastes generated during "cooking," clan labs present very significant health risks to

Clandestine drug labs, especially meth labs, present health risks to narcotics investigators and others. DEA agents, dressed in hazardous materials gear, photograph meth taken from a clan lab in Ohio.

narcotics investigators, other law enforcement personnel, firemen, the public, and the environment. When a clan lab is discovered, law enforcement personnel have to secure the operation. Many lab "cooks" are drug users whose behavior is very erratic. Busting these labs is dangerous not only from the standpoint of the chemicals being used but also because of the people using them. Ketcham and McLeod say that secluded labs are frequently booby-trapped. "Law enforcement first responders have encountered very nasty surprises such as light bulbs loaded with explosives or flammables that detonate or ignite when the switch is flipped; or acid showers triggered by opening a door." Narcotics investigators are trained in the skills necessary to bust these labs safely and to direct their cleanups after the bust.

Hydroponic farming has been used for thousands of years. Hydroponic farms can be small, and they can function with a minimal expenditure of water. Both growth rates and crop yields are higher in hydroponic farming than in traditional dirt farming. Marijuana is one crop that thrives on hydroponic growing techniques. Undercover narcotics investigators frequently receive information about hydroponic marijuana farms and set up operations to close them down. These farms are often found in structures that have very little growing space—such as a grower's home or apartment or even his or her travel trailer. The latest trend in hydroponic marijuana farming is described in an article by MSNBC reporter Stuart Fox. In the article "'Weed on Wheels' Leaves

No Stoner Unturned," he tells about GrowOp Technology Ltd.'s "Big Bud," a trailer filled with "an array of advanced gadgets to create a self-contained, fully mobile, hydroponic marijuana farm. Special air conditioners control the temperature and humidity, robotic lights adjust as the plants grow and users can monitor their operation through their iPhones." He goes on to say that GrowOp Technology is currently working on a system that will allow growers to adjust lights, fans, and other equipment within the Big Bud with their smartphones or computers. It is likely that narcotics investigators will develop surveillance techniques that will allow agents to tap into the iPhones or computers needed to control these operations to identify these marijuana farmers.

CHAPTER SIX

PERKS AND PROBLEMS OF UNDERCOVER NARCOTICS INVESTIGATORS

ndercover narcotics investigators have dangerous jobs, potentially long workweeks, and a lot of on-the-job stress. They are, however, relatively well compensated with good base salaries, overtime pay, and excellent benefit packages.

Salaries and Benefits of Narcotics Investigators

The *Occupational Outlook Handbook*, produced by the Bureau of Labor Statistics and available online at http://www.bls.gov /ooh, offers current information on many professions, including those in law enforcement. Current salaries and benefits are listed at that site. Current salary information can also be obtained on payscale.com. The BLS also gives information about current opportunities in law enforcement and future projections about law enforcement careers. Specific information about salaries and benefits for DEA Special Agents is available on the Web site of the U.S. Office of Personnel

Undercover work frequently requires investigators to work long hours under very stressful conditions. This strain can lead to physical and emotional problems for investigators and can be disruptive to their personal lives.

Management, http://www.opm.gov.

Salaries for narcotics agents vary with the agency that employs them, the states in which they work, their educational backgrounds, and the number of years they have worked. Narcotics agents frequently work irregular hours and may earn a considerable amount of overtime pay. They are usually eligible for a good benefit package that includes medical insurance, the option to sign up for a life insurance program, a variety of retirement savings plans, paid sick leave, and paid vacations.

The state of Oregon, for instance, offers medical, dental, and optical insurance plans; various life insurance policies; short- and long-term disability

ENTRAPMENT IS A COMMON LEGAL DEFENSE IN DRUG CASES

An example of a case in which an entrapment defense was successful is discussed on NOLO.com. Mary Anne Berry was charged with selling illegal drugs to an undercover police officer. She had no previous convictions on drug charges. Berry testified, "The drugs were for my personal use. For nearly two weeks the undercover officer stopped by my apartment and pleaded with me to sell her some of my stash because her mom was extremely sick and needed the drugs for pain relief. I kept refusing." After several more visits from the agent, Berry finally sold her some drugs. She was immediately arrested. According to a jury, the undercover agent's repeated entreaties and lies were sufficiently extreme to constitute entrapment. Their not guilty verdict resulted in Berry's release.

plans; and long-term medical care plans. It contributes varying amounts of money to help agents pay the monthly premiums for these plans. Paid vacation days accrue at different rates depending on the number of years a person has held his or her job. For instance, a police detective who has worked for the state for eleven years will accrue twelve hours of paid leave each month. Officers are also eligible for paid sick leave that accrues at eight hours per month. After six months of employment, officers are eligible for enrollment in the Oregon Public Service Retirement Plan. The state contributes the equivalent of 6 percent of an officer's gross salary to his or her retirement plan each month. Officers may also contribute to a 457 deferred compensation plan as a way to save for retirement.

DEA Special Agent Salary and Benefits

The salaries of most federal employees are based on a system called the general schedule of salaries. There are fifteen grades of salary with ten steps within each grade. Current salaries for each grade and each step within the grade are available on the Web site of the federal government's Office of Personnel Management. New DEA agents are hired at either the GS 7 or GS 9 level, depending on their educations and previous job experience. Agents that join the DEA after serving in the military, for instance, or those with advanced college degrees will be hired at the GS 9 level rather than the GS 7 level. At the end of their basic training, special agents receive a 25 percent increase in their base salaries.

DEA agents receive excellent benefit packages. Their benefits include paid vacations and sick leave, training and relocation expenses, coverage under the Federal Employees Retirement System, excellent health benefits, and group life

Having a military background gives DEA recruits an advantage during training at the DEA Academy. Most are also hired at a higher pay grade than recruits from other backgrounds.

insurance coverage. They can also contribute part of their salaries to 401K savings plans and may participate in the Thrift Savings Plan.

The BLS predicts that job opportunities for narcotics investigators as well as other law enforcement personnel will increase at about 7 percent over the next ten years. This is slightly below the national average for all professions.

Potential Legal Pitfalls for Investigators

Undercover operations are primarily undertaken to gather evidence that will lead to the arrest and conviction of drug dealers. Narcotics investigators must work within the law or the dangers they face and the evidence they gather may be for naught. In addition to developing and carrying out excellent operational plans, undercover narcotics investigators must be aware of the legal pitfalls of their jobs that can result in drug dealers going free instead of to jail.

Lawyers for accused drug dealers often claim that their clients have been entrapped. Entrapment can be used as a legal defense by an attorney if agents resort to behaviors such as the use of threats, harassment, or even flattery to induce suspects to buy drugs or to sell them. To use this defense, a lawyer must show that his or her client had no inclination or intention of committing the crime before coming into contact with the undercover agent(s). The lawyer must also show that the drug dealer committed the illegal act because of undo pressures put on him or her by the agent(s).

Another legal concern for under-cover investigators is that they, themselves, must engage in illegal activities to gather evidence and to maintain their covers. This practice is

An estimated 700 kilograms (1,540 lbs.) of cocaine, shown here, was confiscated in a drug bust by DEA Special Agents in Florida. Its monetary value was estimated at $12 million.

called authorized criminality. Elizabeth Joh, professor of law at the University of California at Davis School of Law, discusses authorized criminality in the article "Breaking the Law to Enforce It: Undercover Police Participation in Crime." She says that authorized criminality poses a host of potential harms to undercover agents themselves. It also erodes public trust in law enforcement agents and agencies, and raises issues about what it means to enforce the law. Most authorities recognize, however, that authorized criminality is often the only way undercover agents can do their jobs successfully and safely. It is probable that this issue will continue to be hotly debated in political and legal circles for years to come.

Personal Pitfalls for Undercover Narcotics Investigators

Before embarking on careers as undercover narcotics investigators, would-be agents should be aware of the stressors of the job and the personal pitfalls of the profession. In the introduction to *In Search of Truth and Honor: Reflections of an Undercover Journey Through the Dark Side of the Badge*, written by Detective Joanne Takasato of the Honolulu, Hawaii, Police Department, Dr. Stephen Band, a psychologist and FBI Special Agent, discusses the stressors that are so destructive to some undercover agents. Five of the stressors he identifies are:

- The lack of commitment on the part of those supervising undercover investigators. Agents perceive this as abandonment.
- The necessity of maintaining an undercover role or assumed identity in a hostile environment.
- Maintaining relationships with suspects while anticipating their inevitable betrayal.
- Lack of any break from the mental preparation and role rehearsals required.
- The physical and cultural distance from "home base," from safe and familiar things.

When agents are sufficiently stressed, they may do incredibly self-destructive things. They may become alcoholics. They may begin to sample the drugs with which they are surrounded and become addicted. They may decide to help themselves to some of the money they have been given for drug buys. They may begin to take bribes from drug cartels or drug traffickers. They may even fabricate evidence against innocent people to pad their arrest rates. As a last resort, they may consider or commit suicide.

A growing awareness of the hazards faced by undercover narcotics investigators has resulted in the development of programs within law enforcement agencies to safeguard the well-being of these men and women. Meredith Krause, Ph.D., a psychologist who serves with the FBI's Undercover Safeguard Unit, in the article "Safeguarding Undercover

Employees: A Strategy for Success," says, "Organizational commitment, support and sensitivity are all necessary conditions for effective implementation of a safeguard program. But the undercover employee's willingness to 'buy in' to the program determines its ultimate success."

When asked if the perks of the profession outweigh its problems, the majority of undercover narcotics investigators say yes. It is the satisfaction of making a positive difference in the lives of others that is the single most important perk of this profession.

GLOSSARY

adage An old saying or proverb.

cartel An association of businesses in an international monopoly.

covert Undercover or hidden.

empathetic Sharing in another person's emotions or feelings.

extraordinaire Exceptional or very unusual.

forensic The application of scientific, especially medical, knowledge to legal matters.

hierarchy A group of persons or things arranged in order of ranks or grades.

illicit Improper or unlawful.

intangible Things that are hard to define or characterize.

integrity Honesty or sincerity.

in vogue Fashionable or popular at a given time.

neurologist A medical doctor who specializes in disorders of the nervous system.

patent medicine A medication that claims to produce a cure but that does not work as promised. Examples are Carter's Little Liver Pills and Fletcher's Castoria.

prosthetic Artificial or manufactured.

rampant Out of control or unchecked.

seizure A sudden attack of severe shaking, frequently accompanied by unconsciousness.

self-esteem Self-respect or pride in oneself.

static Unchanging.

surveillance Close observation of someone.

synthetic Manufactured, as opposed to naturally occurring.

FOR MORE INFORMATION

Canadian Police College (CPC)
P.O. Box 8900
Ottawa, ON K1G 3J2
Canada
(613) 993-9580
Web site: http://www.cpc.gc.ca
The CPC provides advanced and specialized training and
    executive development to law enforcement officers from
    all jurisdictions to help them combat crime and increase
    Canadians' safety.

Criminal Intelligence Service Canada (CISC)
CISC Central Bureau
73 Leikin Drive
Ottawa, ON K1A OR2
Canada
(613) 825-7202
Web site: http://www.cisc.gc.ca
CISC represents four hundred law enforcement agencies
    across Canada. It is a leader in the development of an
    integrated and intelligence-led approach to tackling
    organized crime in Canada.

Drug Enforcement Administration (DEA)
8701 Morrissette Drive
Springfield, VA 22152
(202) 307-1000
Web site: http://www.justice.gov/dea
The DEA is the federal agency responsible for enforcing laws and
    regulations governing narcotics and controlled substances.

Federal Bureau of Investigation (FBI)
FBI Headquarters
935 Pennsylvania Avenue NW
Washington, DC 20535-0001
(202) 324-3000
Web site: http://www.fbi.gov
The FBI is the U.S. agency charged with investigating a
    wide range of federal crimes and supports state,
    local, and other law enforcement agencies in protect-
    ing the nation.

International Association of Chiefs of Police (IACP)
515 North Washington Street
Alexandria, VA 22314
(703) 836-6767
Web site: http://www.theiacp.org
The IACP addresses cutting-edge issues confronting law
    enforcement through advocacy programs and research,
    as well as training and other professional services.

International Association of Undercover Officers (IAUO)
142 Banks Drive
Brunswick, GA 31523
(800) 876-5943
Web site: http://www.undercover.org
E-mail: charles@undercover.org
The IAUO was established for the purpose of promoting
    safety and professionalism among undercover officers.

International Association of Women Police (IAWP)
12600 Kavanaugh Lane
Bowie, MD 20715
(301) 464-1402
Web site: http://www.iawp.org

The International Association of Women Police aims to strengthen, unite, and raise the profile of women in criminal justice around the world.

National Narcotic Officers' Associations' Coalition (NNOAC)
P.O. Box 2456
West Covina, CA 91793
(626) 960-3328
Web site: http://www.natlnarc.org
The NNOAC represents individual state narcotics associations. It researches, monitors, and supports legislative initiatives designed to increase the effectiveness of narcotics law enforcement and law enforcement in general.

National Sheriffs' Association (NSA)
NSA Headquarters
1450 Duke Street
Alexandria, VA 22314
(800) 424-7827
Web site: http://www.sheriffs.org
The NSA is dedicated to serving the Office of Sheriff and its affiliates through police education, police training, and general law enforcement information resources.

Royal Canadian Mounted Police (RCMP)
Headquarters Building
73 Leikin Drive
Ottawa, ON K1A OR2
Canada
(613) 993-2232
Web Site: http://www.rcmp-grc.gc.ca
The RCMP is the national, federal, provincial, and municipal policing body of Canada.

U.S. Office of Occupational Statistics and Employment
Bureau of Labor Statistics (BLS)
Postal Square Building (PSB), Suite 2135
2 Massachusetts Avenue NE
Washington, DC 20211
(202) 691-5700
Web site: http://www.bls.gov
This is the nation's foremost source for career information,
    and where you can find the online *Occupational Outlook
    Handbook* (http://www.bls.gov/ooh).

U.S. Office of Personnel Management (OPM)
1900 E Street NW
Washington, DC 20415
(202) 606-1800
Web site: http://www.opm.gov
The mission of the OPM is to support the federal govern-
    ment's ability to have the best workforce possible to do
    the best job possible.

Web Sites

Due to the changing nature of Internet links, Rosen Publishing
has developed an online list of Web sites related to the
subject of this book. This site is updated regularly. Please use
this link to access the list:

http://www.rosenlinks.com/LAW/Narc

FOR FURTHER READING

Bloom, Shelly. *Jackie Grayson, Undercover Narc*. Seattle, WA: CreateSpace, 2011.

Brezina, Corona. *Careers in Law Enforcement*. New York, NY: Rosen Publishing, 2009.

Chappell, Crissa-Jean. *Narc*. Woodbury, MN: Flux, 2012.

Christen, Carol, and Richard Bolles. *What Color Is Your Parachute? For Teens: Discovering Yourself, Defining Your Future*. 2nd ed. New York, NY: Ten Speed Press, 2010.

Damp, Dennis. *The Book of U.S. Government Jobs: Where They Are; What's Available; and How to Complete a Federal Résumé*. 11th ed. McKees Rock, PA: Bookhaven Press, 2011.

Denton, Mark. *Police Oral Boards: The Ultimate Guide to a Successful Oral Board Interview*. Seattle, WA: CreateSpace, 2009.

Ellery, Mark. *Narc!: A John Doyle Mystery*. Bloomington, IN: Xlibris, 2012.

Foster, Raymond, and Tracey Bisconti. *Police Officer Exam for Dummies*. Hoboken, NJ: Wiley Publishing, 2011.

Gammon, Sherry. *Unlovable*. New York, NY: Wordpaintings, 2011

Kasher, Moshe. *Kasher in the Rye: The True Tale of a White Boy from Oakland Who Became a Drug Addict, Criminal, Mental Patient and Then Turned 16*. New York, NY: Grand Central Publishing, 2012.

Lau, Bernie. *Dance with the Devil: The Memoirs of an Undercover Narcotics Detective*. Seattle, WA: CreateSpace, 2011.

Moreni, Lori. *How to Land a Top-Paying Narcotics Detectives Job: Your Complete Guide to Opportunities,*

Résumés and Cover Letters, Salaries, Promotions, What to Expect from Recruiters and More. London, England: Tebbo, 2012.

Newton, Michael. *Drug Enforcement Administration* (Law Enforcement Agencies). New York, NY: Chelsea House Publishers, 2011.

Peak, Ken. *Policing America: Challenges and Best Practices.* 7th ed. New York, NY: Prentice Hall, 2011.

Peterson's. *Teens' Guide to College and Career Planning.* 11th ed. Lawrenceville, NJ: Peterson Publishing, 2011.

Roberts, Jon, and Evan Wright. *American Desperado: My Life as a Cocaine Cowboy.* London, England: Ebury Publishing, 2012.

Ryan, Jason. *Jackpot: High Times, High Seas, and the Sting That Launched the War on Drugs.* Guilford, CT: Lyons Press, 2012.

Sellers, Tim. *The Last Cowboy: The True Story of One of DEA's Most Decorated Undercover Agents.* Charleston, SC: Four Winds Books, 2012.

Slomka, Beverly. *Teens and the Job Game: Prepare Today— Win Tomorrow.* Bloomington, IN: iUniverse, 2011.

Weatherford, Lacey. *Crush.* Seattle, WA: CreateSpace, 2012.

BIBLIOGRAPHY

ABC 4 News. "Demi's Collapse May Have Been Caused by Smoking Spice." Newport Television, January 30, 2012. Retrieved December 15, 2012 (http://www.abc4.com /content/news/top_stories/story/Demis-collapse -may-have-been-caused-by-smoking-Spice).

Baker, Brian, and Whitney Gunter. "Surveillance: Concept and Practice for Fraud, Security, Crime Investigation." International Foundation for Protection of Officers. Retrieved November 26, 2012 (http://www.ifpo.org /articlebank/surveillance.pdf).

Bigler, Taylor. "New Documentary Tackles Financial, Human Costs of War on Drugs." Daily Caller, October 2, 2012. Retrieved November 17, 2012 (http://dailycaller.com /2012/10/02/new-documentary-tackles-financial -human-costs-of-war-on-drugs).

Burton, Thomas. "Undercover Officer Safety." National Executive Institute Associates, 2012. Retrieved December 16, 2012 (http://www.neiassociates.org /undercover-officer-safety).

Douglas, John. *John Douglas's Guide to Landing a Career in Law Enforcement*. New York, NY: McGraw-Hill, 2004.

Doyle, Paul. *Hot Shots and Heavy Hits*. Lebanon, NH: University Press of New England, 2004.

Drug Enforcement Administration. "The People Behind the Badge." Retrieved December 10, 2012 (http://www .getsmartaboutdrugs.com).

Ferris State University. "Internship Experience at Saginaw DEA Field Office Provides Real Experience for Snowden." August 2012. Retrieved November 24, 2012 (http:// www.ferris.edu/HTMLS/news/archives/2012/august /snowden.html).

Fox, Holly. "Filmmaker Conceals Camera in Prosthetic Eye."
    MSNBC, December 18, 2012. Retrieved December 19,
    2012 (http://www.msnbc.msn.com/id/29637477).

Hoberman, Sarah. "Real Life '21 Jump Street': Undercover
    Cop Returns to High School." ABC News, March 29,
    2012. Retrieved October 9, 2012 (http://abcnews.go
    .com/blogs/headlines/2012/03/real-life-21-jump-street
    -undercover-cop-returns-to-high-school).

Joh, Elizabeth. "Breaking the Law to Enforce It: Undercover
    Police Participation in Crime." *Stanford Law Review*,
    February 24, 2010. Retrieved November 26, 2012
    (http://legalworkshop.org/2010/02/24/breaking-the-law
    -to-enforce-it-undercover-police-participation-in-crime).

Ketcham, Glenn, and Vince McLeod. "The Safety Guys:
    Introduction to Clandestine Drug Laboratories. A Serious
    Health and Safety Concern." June/July 2007. Retrieved
    December 8, 2012 (http://www.wvdhhr.org/rtia/pdf
    /the%20safety%20guys2.pdf).

Krause, Meredith. "Safeguarding Undercover Employees: A
    Strategy for Success." *FBI Law Enforcement Bulletin*,
    August 2008. Retrieved November 27, 2012 (http://
    www2/fbi.gov.publications/leb/2008/august2008leb.htm).

Lieberman, Brian. "Ethical Issues in the Use of Confidential
    Informants for Narcotics Operations." *PoliceChief*, June
    2007. Retrieved November 21, 2012 (http://www
    .policechiefmagazine.org).

Logue, Darin. "The Hidden Badge: The Undercover Narcotics
    Operation." February 1, 2008. Retrieved December 16,
    2012 (http://www.officer.com/article/10249130/the
    -hidden-badge-the-undercover-narcotics-operation).

Marrone, Anthony. "Criminal Justice Student Interns with
    the Drug Enforcement Administration." Wichita State
    University, December 3, 2011. Retrieved November 24,
    2012 (http://www.wichita.edu/thisis/wsunews/news
    /?nid=1309).

Remsberg, Charles. "The Art of Darkness: Keys to Surviving Undercover." PoliceOne, September 2008. Retrieved November 26, 2012 (http://www.PoliceOne.com).

Rice, Lew. *DEA Special Agent: My Life on the Front Line.* Pittsburgh, PA: Dorrance Publishing, 2008.

Sellers, Timothy. "The Last Cowboy." 2012. Retrieved December 10, 2012 (http://www.thelastcowboy.com /Biography.html).

Sipes, Charles. "Advice on Becoming a Gang Investigator: Interview with Gary Killam, President of Florida Gang Investigation Association." June 9, 2011. Retrieved December 3, 2012 (http://www .criminaljusticedegreeschools.com/criminal-justice -schools-south-carolina).

Stanard and Associates. "The National Police Officer Selection Test." U.S. Capitol Police, 2009. Retrieved January 17, 2013 (http://www.uscapitolpolice.gov /post_study_guide_09.pdf).

Takasato, Joanne. *In Search of Truth and Honor: Reflections of an Undercover Journey Through the Dark Side of the Badge.* Charleston, SC: Booksurge Publishing, 2009.

University of Colorado, Denver. "Painkiller Abuse by Kids Way Up, Study Finds." October 17, 2012. Retrieved November 5, 2012 (http://consumer.healthday.com /Articleasp?AID--669722#).

Weinblatt, Richard. "10 Tips for Mastering the Police Oral Board." Policelink, May 29, 2008. Retrieved December 9, 2012 (http://policelink.monster.com/benefits/articles /26352-10-tips-for-mastering-the-police-oral-board).

INDEX

About the Author

Linda Bickerstaff, M.D., has written several books for young adults, including *Cocaine: Coke and the War on Drugs*. This book, and caring for several young people injured in drugged driving accidents, prompted her to expand her knowledge of the evils of illegal drugs and those who sell them. She has great admiration for men and women who are willing to run the risks of undercover narcotics investigators because it's "the right thing to do."

Photo Credits

Cover, pp. 12–13, 15, 16–17, 21, 42–43, 76–77, 84, 88–89, 94–95 © AP Images; pp. 7, 10–11, 32–33, 50–51, 57, 67, 68–69, 72–73, 92–93 Courtesy of the U.S. Drug Enforcement Administration, pp. 6–7, 9, 24, 40, 56, 71, 87 (background image) clearviewstock/Shutterstock.com; pp. 12–13, 15, 16–17, 21, 42–43, 76–77, 84, 88–89, 94–95 © AP Images; pp. 26–27 Hemera/Thinkstock; pp. 30–31 Image Source/Getty Images; pp. 36–37 courtesy of The American Legion, Department of Pennsylvania; p. 41 Kevork Djansezian/Getty Images; pp. 48–49 Scott Olson/Getty Images; pp. 58–59 Globo/Getty Images; pp. 64–65 Izabela Habur/E+/Getty Images; pp. 80–81 Photo by Mark Allen Johnson/ZUMA Press; cover and interior pages background textures Alex Gontar/Shutterstock.com, Eky Studio/Shutterstock.com, Andreas Liem/Shutterstock.com.

Designer: Michael Moy; Editor: Kathy Kuhtz Campbell; Photo Researcher: Marty Levick